Blue Module Leader Training Workbook (F-Edition)
World Class Training for Tomorrow's World Leaders

*Congratulations on being selected to participate in the **Lead**Now Blue Faith-Based Training Module. This workbook includes reminders of your training session activities, Leadership Challenges that you're to do at home, and other useful ideas for leading. Plus, we've put important pages for your parents to read, so be sure you ask them to read the pages in the back. But the real training comes as you interact with your team members, Koaches and Trainers, as you develop your leadership potential.*

In the Blue Module, you'll be learning four of the sixteen most desired qualities of a leader:
- *Integrity: What it means to be a leader others trust.*
- *Confidence: Why courage is important to the team.*
- *Recruit: How to get to gather a team and assign roles.*
- *Vision: What it means see the end result that inspires others.*

Plus, you'll see how God interacts with leaders. We encourage you to go over these notes with a parent or guardian after each club meeting, to help you retain even more of what you learned and maybe even teach him/her about leading effectively as well.

This is your workbook, so feel free to write other leadership ideas on the pages, attach articles, and reflect on what you're thinking about being an effective, ethical leader. Be sure to work on your Leadership Challenge and bring back the signed page to the next club meeting.

*We're proud to have you on the **Lead**Now Team!*

Trainer's name _____

Contact info _____

LeadYoung. Curriculum

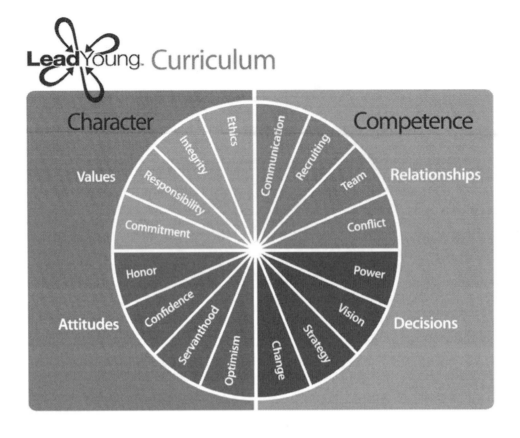

Leader qualities emphasized in this module:

Integrity (Character-Values)
Confidence (Character-Attitudes)
Recruiting (Competency-Relationships)
Vision (Competency-Decisions)

ISBN-13: 978-1477514368
ISBN-10: 1477514368

A letter to you from the founder of KidLead:

We believe in you. That is why you have been invited to participate in a very unique training opportunity, to become an effective, ethical leader. A lot of people may not think you can achieve a lot, because you're so young. But we think of you quite differently. We believe that you have the potential to not only change the world in years to come, but you can start doing it now. That's why we titled this **Lead**Young Training System program, "**Lead**Now!"

Leadership is a unique and valuable ability, to influence people to work together for common goals that help others. As a leader, you are a servant to those you lead and to those who will benefit from what your team accomplishes. As a servant leader, you'll have to make some difficult decisions. You may need to sacrifice and put the needs of others before your own. This requires courage, but will be worth it.

Throughout history, leaders have made good and bad decisions. Bad leaders hurt people through the way they use their power and influence. Good leaders help people by how they use theirs. We want you to become a good leader. You won't be perfect. None of us are. But you will learn how to be an effective, ethical leader, and that starts now, while you're still young. The cartoon graphic introducing each of the four concepts in this module, shows a leader with a heart. This means that leaders must lead with heart, an inner drive to help others.

Our dream is that through the training you'll receive through our **Lead**Young Training Systems, you'll become a world changer. Your Certified Trainer(s) and Koaches believe in you. We take this training very seriously and have put a lot of time and work into making it both fun and effective. But the key is what you do with what you learn. We hope you'll not only become a great leader, but that you'll help others learn to lead as well. The best way to do this is to model it; show them. While many people see a kid when they look at you, we see a leader. You're still young, but we want you to **Lead** Now!

Believing in you,

Alan E. Nelson, EdD
Founder of LeadYoung Training Systems
Los Angeles, CA

Table of Contents

Blue Module Club Expectations

1. *Good leaders learn to listen.*
   a. Team members have good ideas; we need to listen so we can learn from others.
   b. Raise your hand in your team when you want to talk.
   c. Look at your team members when they're speaking.

2. *Good leaders get involved.*
   a. Leaders learn by doing, so be sure to participate.
   b. People watch what leaders do, so be sure to model involvement.

3. *Good leaders honor others.*
   a. We say things in a way that help people sense their value.
   b. We all like to learn where we feel like we're respected and liked.

4. *Good leaders can follow, too.*
   a. Good leaders know how to respect their superiors (leading up).
   b. Show respect to your Team Leaders when they provide instructions.

5. *Good leaders are responsible.*
   a. Bring this workbook to every training session.
   b. Do your best to get your mom/dad/guardian to get you to club meetings on time (if that applies).
   c. If you'll be gone or late, let your Trainer know if possible.
   d. Every week you'll be given a Leadership Challenge that should take 15-20 minutes and that your parent or guardian is asked to sign.

I understand and agree to do these to the best of my ability.

Signature: _____

Leader Quality: Integrity

Our leader here is framing his heart, because integrity is at the very center of ethical leading. The word *integrity* is from a term meaning complete, whole. This quality refers to a person who does what he says and is not divided between what he values and how he acts.

Integrity has to do with honesty, being trustworthy, and being dependable. Although we believe this is an important quality for everyone, it is essential for leaders. When a leader lacks integrity, people don't trust her. That makes leading very difficult, because trust is the glue that holds a team together. Leaders who lack integrity are untrustworthy and undependable. History is full of leaders who've deceived, cheated, and lied to people. As a result, many people have been hurt.

As a young leader with integrity, you take what you say very seriously because you know you need to follow through with action. In this section, you'll learn what leadership integrity is along with its importance.

Blue Module Lesson #1
Values: Integrity

Key Concept: Teams need to trust their leaders. **Good leaders do what they say.**

Verse: James 5:12 (Mean what you say.)

Lesson #1: *Team Building:* Developing a name, slogan, and team machine helped us get to know others and work together. Integrity literally means "whole." Leaders help teams unite as one.

Lesson #2: *Ladder of Integrity:* We discovered the importance of trust as we climbed across a horizontal ladder, supported by others. Faith relies on God's integrity. A leader's integrity develops trust.

Lesson #3: *Investment Activity:* We learned how a leader's words and actions influence whether people believe them or not. Good leaders are trustworthy, so that people invest in what they say.

Notes: One main idea I want to apply from this session:

Lesson #1
Leadership Challenge

Instructions: Write or list at least two examples of integrity, or a lack of integrity, by a leader with his/her company or team. This may be a news article from a magazine, newspaper, or the Internet, regarding a leader who said one thing but did another and could not be trusted. This might also be something you do as a leader or observe someone else doing, such as a parent, teacher, or another person. Be sure to think of a leadership situation involving three or more people, not just an individual who lies or doesn't follow through alone.

Signature of parent/guardian _____

Be ready to share this at the next training session.

Leader Biography

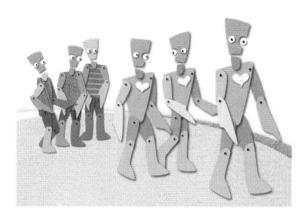

Integrity is an important quality to possess as an individual, but it is essential as a leader. A person with integrity is trustworthy. Leaders need trust to lead, because when people feel that you are undependable, don't do what you say, or that you'll betray them, they won't follow.

One of the best examples of leadership integrity is the life of Joseph. When he was a young man, around your age, his jealous brothers gave him to some traveling merchants and then lied to his father, saying he'd been killed. Joseph became a servant in a leader's home in Egypt. The leader trusted him. But because he was strong and good looking, the leader's wife tried to seduce him. Joseph displayed integrity and ran. She felt embarrassed, so she lied about him to her husband, who threw him into prison. But even then, Joseph maintained his integrity and proved himself trustworthy and dependable.

After leaving prison, Joseph became a very powerful leader in Egypt, because Pharaoh discovered that Joseph could be trusted. When his brothers came to get grain during a famine, he saw them, but they didn't recognize him. Instead of getting angry and having them put in prison or killed, he helped them. Joseph forgave them (Genesis 50). The family then moved to Egypt to live, because of Joseph's kindness. Even though they betrayed him, he took care of them, because Joseph had integrity.

Although having integrity doesn't make you a leader, good leaders possess integrity. A lack of dependability and trust will cause people to doubt you and avoid following you as a leader. Therefore, if you want to lead, do what you say, be honest, and prove yourself dependable.

Blue Module Lesson #2
Values: Integrity

Key Concept: Teams need to trust their leaders. **Good leaders do what they say.**

Verse: Titus 1:7-8 (God expects leaders to be dependable.)

Lesson #1: *Two Truths & A Lie:* Leaders need to be good at telling the truth as well as estimating when people may be deceiving the team. Honesty is vital to people trusting leaders. Plus, God expects it.

Lesson #2: *Cup Challenge:* Leaders can't always assume everything is as it appears. They must check the facts. People are depending on us to do what is right.

Lesson #3: *Basketball Marshmallow:* Leaders need to be dependable and honest. We experienced what it is like when someone we trust was dishonest.

Notes: One main idea I want to apply from this session:

Lesson #2

L.E.A.D. # H.O.N.E.S.T.Y. Mini-Lesson

A word related to integrity is honest. An honest leader has integrity.

High standards: a leader with integrity makes good ethical choices; keeps the rules

Open to inspection: a leader of integrity is willing to let others hold them accountable

Not a loner: a leader of integrity lets other people know them, because relationships help us live properly

Example for others: a leader of integrity is willing to keep the standards he or she expects from others

Says & does: a leader of integrity does what he or she says; your walk matches your talk

Truthful: doesn't try to deceive others or hide the facts from the rest of the team, when it will help the team get better, even if it's not easy truth

Lesson #2

Leadership Challenge

Instructions: Interview your mom, dad, teacher, coach or another adult, and ask them to tell you a story about a time in their lives when either they know lacked integrity or even when they did something that lacked integrity that affected someone else.

Write the notes of this story here so you can briefly retell the story to your team.

Signature of parent/guardian _____

Be ready to share this at the next training session.

Notes

Leader Quality: Confidence

Our leader here is raising her arms, a sign of victory and excitement. Notice how her attitude is affecting the others, so that they too feel confident. Confidence, like many attitudes, has a way of influencing the entire team. That's why leaders need to keep their fears to themselves and communicate boldness and courage to others.

People don't like to follow leaders who lack courage, because it doesn't give them a sense that they know where they're going or that they'll accomplish much. During every significant team effort, there come times when people question the process and the outcome. Fear can overwhelm a team. A leader's courage and boldness helps a team get through these difficult times. Obviously, the best confidence is based on experience, skill, and knowledge, so good leaders strive to make sure their confidence is well grounded, not fake.

In this section, we're going to learn about the importance of confidence and how it affects a team, as well as trying to improve this quality in you as a leader.

Blue Module Lesson #3
Attitudes: Confidence

Key Concept: Teams seek reassurance. **A good leader believes in the team and task.**

Verse: Philippians 4:13 (You can do all things through Christ.)

Lesson #1: *Card Line-Up:* We discovered that one way to increase confidence is by increasing practice and experience. Leaders help teams accomplish this, even if it's not fun.

Lesson #2: *People Horseshoes:* By being blindfolded, we discovered how limited perceptions and feedback reduce our confidence and performance. Leaders create confidence by communicating well. Faith is trusting God, even when we can't see Him.

Lesson #3: *Origami:* We saw how having complete information is important to confidence and success. Leaders are responsible for providing the right information.

Notes: One main idea I want to apply from this session:

Lesson #3

Leadership Challenge

Instructions: Leaders need to be able to express courage and confidence in front of their team, if their team is going to feel confident and courageous. This challenge involves interacting with one or more adults who you don't know, in order to gain experience to increase your confidence. Following are examples. Pick one or come up with a similar one, as long as it seems challenging to you. Write on this page what you did, how you did it, and the results. Report back at the next club meeting. Ask permission from your parent beforehand.

- While shopping, do all the interactions of paying at the register.
- When eating out, be the one who talks to the waiter, orders all the food, and makes any additional requests.
- Ask directions from a gas station attendant.
- Go to a neighbor's house and borrow an egg (or flour, etc.).

Signature of parent/guardian _____

Be ready to share this at the next training session.

Leader Biography

Confidence is a valuable quality to possess as a person, but it is essential if you want to lead. The reason is that the confidence of a leader inspires people on the team to accomplish more, when they feel fearful, unsure, or insecure.

An example of leader confidence is the story of David and Goliath (1 Samuel 17). Goliath was a bully. Bigger than everyone else, he'd come out and make fun of King Saul's army. David was around your age at the time, taking care of his family's sheep, while his brothers served in the army. One day when he was bringing them food, Goliath came out.

David saw that everyone was scared of this giant. He thought, "I can take this guy." David felt confident because he had experience using a slingshot. But when he went out to face Goliath, he expressed additional confidence, faith in God. He said, "I come to you in the name of the Lord." David's slingshot rock hit Goliath in the head, knocking him out, so David ran over and killed him. When the army of Israel saw what happened, they gained confidence so they chased the Philistines and won the battle.

David led here as an unofficial leader, because he did not hold rank in the army. Good leaders realize that at certain times, they can become leaders by being confident. This quality makes others want to follow them. Obviously, being overly confident can work against you, if you act like you can accomplish something when you can't. But in general, the most confident people emerge as leaders in groups, because the team catches their boldness. Good leaders are confident.

Blue Module Lesson #4
Attitudes: Confidence

Key Concept: Teams seek reassurance. **A good leader believes in the team and task.**

Verse: Acts 1:8 (God's Spirit gives us boldness and courage.)

Lesson #1: *We Can Do That:* We discovered how confident we were or were not as we bid against other teams in doing a task. Leaders need to take risks, but reasonable ones.

Lesson #2: *Chariot Races:* We experience how important it is to trust others and have them trust us. Leaders help team members trust each other, just as we depend on God (faith).

Lesson #3: *Card Tower:* We learned how changes can challenge confidence. Leaders help us respond to changes, so that we aren't fearful and can react well as a team.

Notes: One main idea I want to apply from this session:

Lesson #4

 # 5 S's of Confidence Mini-Lesson

1. See their eyes.

(Action: point your first two fingers toward your eyes) **Leaders create confidence when they look their team members in the eyes. When a leader does not look at people in the eyes, this is a sign they cannot be trusted or that they are afraid.**

2. Say the positive.

(Action: thumbs-up sign) **When people are fearful, they start to think about and talk about the negative, what they think will go wrong. Leaders build confidence when they state the positive. This creates hope. Say things such as, "We can do it." "We're going to make it."**

3. Speak up.

(Action: cup hands around mouth like a megaphone) **When we are nervous and fearful, our voice usually constricts and we don't talk loudly. Confident people speak up, so a leader should talk clearly so all can hear.**

4. Smile.

(Action: use your first to fingers to push up the corners of your mouth to form a smile) **Leaders smile, providing assurance to their team, because when people are nervous, smiling is not natural. Smiling shows confidence and provides courage to others.**

5. Stand tall.

(Action: stand on tiptoes) **When we feel afraid, we tend to slump. Standing tall is a subtle way that leaders can show confidence. Stand up with your chest out.**

Lesson #4
Leadership Challenge

Instructions: Leaders need to be able to face their fears if they are going to lead others in attempting tasks that may risk failure, require sacrifice, make them face their own lack of confidence. In this Leadership Challenge, you need to come up with something that you either fear or lack confidence in doing, and then attempt it. Record below what it is you did, when and how you accomplished it, and how it made you feel. You don't have to succeed, but you do need to try, in order to feel the feeling of facing your fears.

Perhaps it is speaking in public, ordering your own food at a restaurant, asking a new person over to play ball or watch a movie, or volunteer to visit an elderly person at a retirement home. So long as it is physically safe, do something you think will challenge your confidence.

What did you do?

Why did it seem difficult for you?

What were the results?

Signature of parent/guardian_____

Be ready to share this at the next training session.

Notes

Leader Quality: Recruiting

Our leader here is inviting someone to join the team. That's because leaders understand the importance of asking people to join them and helping them find a position on the team that matches their strengths with what is needed to achieve the goal.

The "task of ask" is what leaders must do, because finding quality people is not easy. You can't merely hope or wish people will follow you or find a place on the team where they'll be effective. That's the leader's job. A good leader goes after the right people and then invites them to be on the team. This means facing the fear of rejection, because the person may say "no." But once on the team, it's also the leader's responsibility to help that person succeed by finding a place that matches his or her abilities.

In these training sessions, we're going to focus on the importance of recruiting a team, along with matching abilities with tasks, so that you can reach your potential as a group.

Blue Module Lesson #5
Relationships: Recruiting

Key Concept: People want to win. **A good leader helps people use their strengths.**

Verse: Romans 12:4-8 (God gives people unique abilities.)

L.E.A.D. Lesson #1: *Design Recruiter:* We learned the importance of talent as we selected a winning paper airplane design to help us as a team. Leaders don't have to have the best ideas, but must help find them.

L.E.A.D. Lesson #2: *Puzzled:* We discovered what it means to find the right people, recruit them, and then complete the task of completing a puzzle. Leaders match people with tasks, to help them succeed.

L.E.A.D. Lesson #3: *The Relay:* We saw how placing people in the best roles makes sense in accomplishing tasks such as the relay race. God expects leaders to help people achieve, through using their talents.

Notes: One main idea I want to apply from this session:

Lesson #5
Leadership Challenge

Instructions: People want to be useful when they're a part of a team. That means that leaders need to understand the tasks that need to be accomplished as well as the abilities required to complete them, and find the people with those abilities. Start with the task and break it into parts. Select one of the three following situations and come up with at least five tasks required to accomplish it. When you divide a project into smaller tasks, it's easier to recruit people because you know what you want them to accomplish, and they feel more successful.

Option 1: Putting on a garage sale
Option 2: Cleaning up a vacant lot in the neighborhood
Option 3: Collecting canned goods for a food drive for a homeless shelter

Task #1:

Task #2:

Task #3:

Task #4:

Task #5:

Signature of parent/guardian_____

Be ready to share this at the next training session.

Leader Biography

Recruiting involves inviting people to be in certain positions on a team, so that you can accomplish a lot. Although everyone can understand the importance of recruiting, this is what good leaders do well.

One of the best recruiters in the Bible was Paul. We know this because as he traveled around, he started new churches. He found out who could teach, who could host a group in their home, and who should be in charge. He also taught a lot about team building, so we know he understood the idea of recruiting.

For example, in chapter twelve of 1 Corinthians and Romans, Paul talks about different gifts and abilities that people possess, like parts of the body. God gives people unique abilities. No one can do everything. Just as a soccer coach figures out who should be goalie, who is good at offence, and the best defenders, everyone's not the same. Paul taught that some people are good at praying, others at making people feel welcome, and still others at teaching. In Ephesians chapter 4, he says "that if your gift is leadership, do it well."

Good leaders recruit, meaning they know that tasks are needed to accomplish the goal and then asking people with those talents, to go to those positions. A lot of people in church don't understand this, so they try to get anyone to fill a position. But Paul realized that if you put nice but ungifted people into positions, the team won't function well. Even though every task is different, everyone has value.

So, whether you're recruiting for an athletic team, music band, or school club, think about who can do what and then ask those people. That's recruiting.

Blue Module Lesson #6
Relationships: Recruiting

Key Concept: People want to win. **A good leader helps people use their strengths.**

Verse: 1 Corinthians 12:14 (Leaders unite individuals to work together.)

Lesson #1: *Sock It to Me:* We experienced why recruiting more people on a team can make a difference in its performance (catching socks). Leaders strive to gain as many members as are needed.

Lesson #2: *Draw It:* We discovered that it is difficult to do well when you don't have talent in the right areas (such as drawing with our toes). Leaders align tasks with talents.

Lesson #3: *Team Recruiter:* We worked together as a team to put an imaginary company staff together (even if they were cards). Jesus recruited his team. We need to do the same as leaders.

Notes: One main idea I want to apply from this session:

Lesson #6

L.E.A.D 4 Keys in Recruiting Mini-Lesson

- **1. Team Chemistry Is Important**

People need to get along and honor each other. A leader's task is to help create an atmosphere of friendship, trust, and even fun, so that people want to belong to your team and work together.

- **2. Pursuing the Win Is Important**

Just getting together is insufficient. Leadership is about pursuing a cause to accomplish a task. While you may not always win, trying to win and desiring to achieve is important, and something the leader needs to help create.

- **3. Valuing Everyone Is Important**

No matter who is on your team, each person needs to be treated with honor. Even when you need to confront a person, do it with honor. People can sense when they are truly cared for or merely being used.

- **4. Tapping Talent Is Important**

Your job as a leader is to invite people to the team who can help you accomplish the task. Then it's to help each person find a place where they can use their talent or skill that will help the team the most.

Lesson #6
Leadership Challenge

The Task of Ask

Instructions: One of the most challenging things for a leader is asking people to help. This requires taking a risk of being turned down or negotiating so the other person gets something out of it. If a leader does not do this well, the team will not be effective. Your assignment is to practice the "task of ask" by recruiting people two times (not family members who will automatically do it for you). Record who you "recruited" and what you asked the person to do, even if you were not successful. Here are examples:

- *Ask a neighbor whom you don't know well (with your parent's permission), to give you an item such as an egg, stamp, canned food for the homeless, or cup of milk.*
- *Recruit at least two friends to join you in doing a good deed for a neighbor or to clean trash from a nearby lot.*
- *Ask a grocery store clerk to help you find a certain food item.*
- *Recruit an entire family you know to come over for a meal.*

Person #1 recruited: _____

Task _____

What did you learn from this?

Person #2 recruited: _____

Task _____

What did you learn from this?

Signature of parent/guardian_____

Be ready to share this at the next training session.

LeadNow. Blue Faith-Based Module Leader's Workbook
©2012, 2021   www.kidlead.com

Notes

Leader Quality: Vision

Our leader here is viewing the mountain through binoculars. The leader's most unique responsibility is to help the team know where it is headed. The leader must keep his eye on the big picture, or the end goal. A vision is not only what you want to achieve together, but why you want to achieve it.

A vision must be communicated by a leader so it inspires people to follow. Great visions in history involved discovering new territories, landing a person on the moon, fighting bad leaders, and establishing organizations to help people. A good vision helps people see in their minds what it is the team is going to accomplish together. The ability to say it clearly and powerfully is not easy, but good leaders do this well. A leader must also help the team develop a strategy and plan, but vision is what motivates us to work together and sacrifice.

These activities are going to help you learn what a vision is, how to communicate it, and why it is so important to leading. By the end, we hope you'll be able to analyze visions as well as communicate your own effectively.

Blue Module Lesson #7
Decisions: Vision

Key Concept: Teams thrive on inspiration. **A good leader imagines the victory before it happens.**

Verse: Jeremiah 29:11 (God has a vision for us to succeed.)

Lesson #1: *Million $ Project:* We practiced drawing and presenting a vision for a project that would help others. Leaders communicate the future of what can be.

Lesson #2: *Fashion Balloons:* We used our creativity to design a balloon clothing item and then sell it to potential buyers. Leaders cast the vision for new ideas and help people create new things.

Lesson #3: *Movie Director:* We used our imagination to develop a movie plot, seeing the end result and then describing it. The Bible shows us how God designs scripts for his people. Leaders direct a team's path.

Notes: One main idea I want to apply from this session:

Lesson #7
L.E.A.D V.I.S.I.O.N. Mini-Lesson

View the end...

Visualize what the dream will look like when it's done: a building, a gold medal around your neck, being in shape, a World Series pennant or trophy.

Imagine the benefits...

What will people get out of it—freedom, or money, or happiness, or a meaning, or purpose?

Sell the importance...

Why is this so important? Lives are at stake. No one has done this before. The future depends on it.

Inspire involvement... We need you. There's a place for you.
This can be your dream too.

Own it yourself...

I'm willing to sacrifice, to be involved, to die for this cause. Join me in this effort.

Need it now...

We can't wait. We need to do this now, time is of the essence.

Lesson #7
Leadership Challenge

Presidential Speech: Your job is to write a speech for the President of the United States, to present to the American people, casting a vision for one of the three topics. We want you to write this speech and then present it to your team at the next club meeting, as if they were the American public. Your goal is to inspire your listeners to action. Keep it to around 50 words.

- Idea 1: Why we should build a rocket to take people to Mars.
- Idea 2: How we can reduce poverty in Africa.
- Idea 3: Why we should develop kids as future leaders.

Signature of Parent _____

Be ready to share this at the next training session.

Leader Biography

Vision is uncommon among non-leaders. Although it's good for everyone to have personal goals and be self-motivated, good leaders communicate a picture that motivates people to accomplish the task. Although you can have a vision and not be a leader, leaders who accomplish the most are what we call visionary.

Two examples of visionary leaders in the Bible are Joshua and Caleb. Moses selected 12 men to spy out the land of Canaan, where the nation of Israel was headed after leaving Egypt as slaves (Numbers 13 & 14). But when the men returned, only Joshua and Caleb gave a visionary report. The other spies reported about giants in the land, making the people afraid so that they turned against Moses. Joshua and Caleb said, "No, there are giants, but we can defeat them. Plus, there are so many good things in the land, we should go there."

In spite of Joshua and Caleb's vision, the people still did not want to go. By nature, people tend to avoid the unknown, which means staying the way they are even if it is not good. That's why the vision of a leader must be clear, confident, and filled with hope. Even though Joshua and Caleb communicated their vision, the negative attitudes of the other spies created so much fear that the people turned from the Promised Land. God let them wander in the desert for forty years.

After that, Joshua became the main leader and moved the people into Canaan. Leaders who are good at communicating vision usually have followers. Vision is not easy to develop. But the better you get at helping people look past the giants to what can be accomplished, the more they will want to follow you.

Blue Module Lesson #8
Decisions: Vision

Key Concept: Teams thrive on inspiration. **A good leader imagines the victory before it happens.**

Verse: Matthew 17:20 (Faith increases our vision. See it big.)

Lesson #1: *Vision Speeches:* We heard famous speeches that created a sense of vision for our country. Leaders speak with vision that inspires others to follow.

Lesson #2: *Game Invention:* We created an original game and then made our sales pitch to "company executives" to get them to invest. Leaders must help people see things, before they are reality.

Lesson #3: *The Ending:* (Optional if time allows): We decided the ending to a story and explained what we'd pictured in our minds. Leaders help us see a preferred future, just like God.

Notes: One main idea I want to apply from this session:

Blue Lesson #8
Leadership Challenge

Blue Module Review: Wow, what a great experience. Good leaders reflect on what they learn, so take time now to write answers to the following questions:

What is one thing you learned about leading from this module?

Which of the Leadership Challenges stand out to you and why?

Which of the L.E.A.D. activities was memorable and why?

How do you think you're a better leader now?

What fellow Leader did you come to appreciate in this module and why?

Blue Module Key Concepts Review

Integrity: Good leaders do what they say.

Confidence: A good believes in the team and task.

Recruiting: A good helps people use their strengths.

Vision: A good leader imagines the victory before it happens.

Signatures

All of you are going to do <u>great</u> <u>things</u> as leaders, and some of you will become famous doing them, so get everyone's signature now!

Leadership Project

INSTRUCTIONS: We encourage every club to do a leadership project after each training module. This allows you to practice skills that you've learned during the training.

Success in a leadership project is not determined by accomplishing the goal, as much as it is how you did in trying to attempt it, what you learned from the experience, and how you did as a leader. So try to think of a plan that is challenging and yet possible.

3 Factors Needed For A Leadership Situation
- ◆ At least three or more people are involved in a task.
- ◆ There is a goal to accomplish (it is measurable).
- ◆ There is a need for change, improvement or new direction (not just maintaining).

This project should not be run by adults whereby students are following them, but rather where each student has an opportunity to lead a team of 3 or more during one part of the project. Following are some things to consider as you plan your project and accomplish it.

You can use this as an outline. Feel free to write your answers to these basic questions, to help you think through a leadership process.

Idea Starters
- What's a need your school or organization has right now?
- What is a current program that you could improve or expand?
- Raise food for a local food bank.
- Collect clothes and donate to the Salvation Army or homeless shelter.
- Raise money for Compassion International or other children's charity.
- Talk to your principal, rabbi, pastor, priest or teacher for a special project in their organization.
- Just keep in mind: safety, time, and ability to be accomplished before the next **Lead**Now module begins.

Strategic Coaching Questions
1. What are possible ways to lead a team in this situation?
2. How does your team intend to accomplish this goal?
3. Who is going to do what?
4. How are you going to monitor your progress?

ADDITIONAL QUESTIONS: These are extra ideas that the project "coach," who is a parent, guardian, teacher, or Trainer can ask you, to help you think through the process. Remember, the adult should not offer solutions, but rather help the Leaders think through the process.

1. What is it you want to accomplish? Write this out in 10-20 words.

2. Break this into smaller tasks and roles?

3. What types of talent do you need to accomplish these?

4. Name any other people you plan to invite to your team.

5. Why did you select these people?

6. How are you going to go about completing this task as a team? Break it into smaller tasks or roles. Use additional space as needed.

7. What are the key tasks and who is going to do what task or role?

8. What resources do you need to accomplish this?

9. How do you plan to get these resources?

10. When do you want to have it completed? Are there any deadlines before this?

11. How will you organize your people to work as a team?

12. What challenges or problems might you face and how might you solve these? In other words, if this project failed, what would be the possible causes and how can you work to address these before you begin?

13. How will you measure the success of this project?

14. What else haven't you thought about and how can you go about finding out what you don't know?

LEADERSHIP PROJECT REVIEW
Complete this after your project is completed

1. What was it that you attempted (20-30 words):

1. What well about your project?

2. How did your team work together or not?

3. What was a challenge or problem you faced during the task?

4. What might you do differently next time you lead, or if you had to do this again?

5. What did you personally learn about leading from this project?

We'd like to get a copy of your team's project in the KidLead offices, so we can share it on the website for others to see. Send to the contact info on the website or to: info@kidlead.com.

Sitch Leading

When you're the Team Leader, you have 4 basic approaches you can select, based on the situation.* Following is a brief description of each, along with the positives (strengths) and negatives (weaknesses) of each style

TELL

☐ *Tell* **everyone what you think is the best way**

☐ **Let each person know what to do**

☐ **Be clear and be direct (but nice)**

\+ Direct & clear, especially useful in a crisis
\+ Saves time, when speed is important
\- You appear bossy & people don't like bossy leaders
\- You may not see something important because you limit ideas

SELL

☐ **Ask for ideas from the team**

☐ **Select the idea you think is best**

☐ *Sell* **it to the team and provide directions**

\+ Team members feel more like they are heard
\+ Sharing ideas can help the team avoid mistakes
\- If you only *sell* your ideas, people may think you're insincere
\- Can be challenging to keep from moving to Tell or Gel

GEL

☐ **Brainstorm ideas with team members**

☐ **Discuss the best strategies**

☐ *Gel* **the team as you build consensus (unity)**

\+ The team feels their ideas are heard, increasing commitment
\+ The best ideas often emerge because they are discussed
\- This can take a lot of time and you may lose an opportunity
\- Sometimes the best ideas get lost in the process

DEL

☐ *Del***egate authority to someone else to lead**

☐ **You are still responsible for the outcome**

☐ **(In LeadNow we delegate tasks, not leading)**

\+ Team members feel empowered and trusted
\+ This is a good way to develop others as leaders
\- This can be a way a leader avoids responsibility (fearful/lazy)
\- True delegation includes authority, which increases risk

Leader & Team Player

When you're the leader, it's your job to initiate teamwork. Here are some ideas (L.E.A.D.):

Listen to your team's ideas
· "Our goal is to …, so what are your ideas?"
· "All right, what other ideas are there?"
· "Thanks for sharing, now let's get a plan."

Establish the plan
· Select the ideas that seem the best.
· "Here's the direction I think we should take…"
· "This is how we'll get this done… "

Assign tasks
· "Who wants to do what?"
· "Ashley, why don't you…."
· "Jesse, we need you to…"

Determine the progress
· If things are going well:
  • "Hey, nice job, team!" "Great work, (name a team member)."
· If things could go better:
  • "Let's work faster, time is running out." "Wait a second, let's rethink our plan."

You're not ready to be a good leader until you know how to be a good team member. This includes knowing how to influence your leader and teammates at times. Here are some ideas on how to do this (T.E.A.M.):

Take directions well
· "We're listening; what's the plan?"
· "What can I do to help?"
· "Okay, we'll do it."

Express your ideas positively
· "What if we tried it this way?"
· "Could I share an idea?"
· "Here's another option to consider."

Affirm your leader
· "Great job."
· "Thanks for leading us."
· "Hey, we did it!"

Make the team glad you're on it.
· "We can do it; let's pull together."
· "Nice job everyone."
· "I'm willing to try.

What's Next?

If you're between the ages of 10-13 and have not yet completed all 4 **Lead**Now modules, then your next step is hopefully another module. But if you've completed all 4 **Lead**Now modules and have turned 14, or if you've moved on to high school, then your next step is **Lead**Well, a similar but age-appropriate training program for teens. Plus, we even have a book just for you, called **Lead**Young. Ask your trainer about this program. You'll learn a lot. Plus, you'll love it.

The World's Finest Teen Leadership Training Curriculum

In this 238-page book, written for 14-23-year olds, Dr. Nelson deals with the issues facing young leaders. This is the first organizational leadership book ever written for teens, addressing young adult challenges such as having little formal experience and no position of authority. You'll learn how to gain power from various sources, how to lead up and laterally, and what you need to focus on for future success. Nearly every book on leadership is for adults, so we knew something different was needed.

This book goes along with the **Lead**Well training program, but can also be obtained at www.amazon.com. For bulk quantities of 10 or more, contact us at info@kidlead.com or at www.leadyoungtraining.com.

Parent & Guardian Section

Student Leader, make sure your parent reads the next 4 pages. It will help you.

Dear Parent,

*Your **Lead**Young Certified Trainer and I are thrilled that your child and you are involved in **Lead**Now. Our vision is that this would become a national and global leadership development movement for raising effective, ethical leaders. We know that it comes down to providing an excellent experience for each young person and it can't be done without the involvement of supportive parents. Whether this is your first module or you're a returning family, please review these materials.*

While some parents may see this as just one more extracurricular activity, we take this program very seriously. We've invested 1000s of hours in testing and retesting activities, based on some of the best executive and teaching methodologies. The curriculum wheel will show you what your young leader is learning.

Here are three things you can do to enhance your child's training experience:

ONE: Sit through at least one entire training session, observing from the sidelines. You'll get a feel of what your Leader is experiencing that will better equip you to talk to him/her about each meeting. Review the content in this workbook, to give you some talking points. This can go far in reinforcing the training being done during the training session.

TWO: In each club meeting, your Leader will be given a "Leadership Challenge," a 15-20 minute activity that is designed to help him/her apply the principle taught during the previous training session. Your responsibility is to "sign off" on the Leadership Challenge page in this workbook, once your child has accomplished this. Please make this a positive, coaching experience, not "homework." You may even want to do the challenge on your own and compare notes with your young Leader.

THREE: Periodically, your Trainer(s) should be offering parent training. Ask your Trainer about the 1-hour, "Developing Your Church to Lead" workshop, and the 2-hour "Raising a Leader" clinic. We highly encourage you to read the book, "KidLead: Growing Great Leaders." We want to help you raise a great leader in addition to the training sessions. We've noticed that without this training, parents often slow down the development of their young leader, without realizing it.

Together, we can develop the leadership potential of your child, resulting in a better world.

Yours truly,

Alan E. Nelson, Ed.D.

5 Coaching Ideas for Home Use

*Although we provide more in depth training in the **Lead**Now parent training workshops, the book "KidLead: Growing Great Leaders" and the website, here are 5 quick tips to maximize your young Leader's training at home. These parenting skills specifically focus on leadership development.*

1. **Think coach, not parent**. There are many ways of parenting. Three common but ineffective ways include:
    a. Power: yelling, put downs, intimidation, "Be quiet. I'm talking!"
    b. Suggesting: providing solutions for your child; "Why don't you… "
    c. Explaining: reasoning but without the consequences; "Here's why… "
   But the most effective parenting and coaching involve teaching your child how to problem solve, requiring you to ask more questions than give answers.
    d. Problem Solving: explore feelings, solutions and consequences.
        i. How do you think your friend felt when you said that?
        ii. What are some possible ways to solve this problem?
        iii. What might happen if we did it this way?

2. **Give your Leader room to fly**. Leaders learn by experience, meaning you'll want to hold back, letting them develop and experiment with their own solutions. This takes more time and patience, but it is the best way. Let your Leader make choices that the entire family experiences. Put him in charge of a family task. Let her set the agenda in specific situations, as you follow.

3. **Turn daily tasks into leadership situations for gaining skills**. For example, instead of assigning dinner chores, empower your Leader to oversee the meal, including deciding what to eat, making sure the food is available and on budget, determining who'll prepare it, what time everyone can eat, and who'll clean up. This turns a simple chore into a true leadership experience.

4. **Create leadership projects in your regular schedule**. Three things are needed to establish a legitimate leadership project:
    a. A clear goal (but not all the details of how to achieve it).
    b. At least 2-3 people in addition to the Leader.
    c. Debrief time after, to discuss how things went and what s/he learned.

5. **Reinforce desired behaviors**. Catch your Leader doing something well and notice it. Allow the freedom to fail in leadership projects. Discuss failures as matter of fact. Celebrate taking risks. The best way to create positive attitudes and action is to affirm your leader and avoid overreacting when the plan doesn't happen as you like.

By creating a positive learning environment at home, where you share opportunities for leading among family members, you give your leaders a 10-20 year head start on other leaders.

8 Great Training Benefits

Identifies leadership aptitude: *Lead*Now identifies youth with leadership aptitude. Through the *Social Influence Survey* and live training opportunities, we can invite those with natural leadership potential to experience more concentrated training.

Unique combination of character and skill training: The 10-13 year old *window* allows us to target leaders when their cognitions are developed to learn complex social skills and their character is still pliable. By combining character and competency, we lessen the risk of leaders compartmentalizing their ethics from leadership decisions that is the root of many organizational scandals.

Concentrated practical experience: Over the course of our 4 training modules, participants experience approximately 100 activities related to various aspects of leading. These are accomplished in teams, among peers, with adult coaching and feedback. That is a lot of supervised experience, utilizing accelerated learning methods that research says heightens retention. Just as athletes use muscle memory to improve, repetitive leading heightens skill and confidence.

Provides a 15-25 year head start: Most formal leadership training does not begin until the ages of 25-35, when certain employees are identified as potential leaders and provided seminars, training events and mentoring. *Lead*Now's early development provides a significant head start. In his book, *Outliers*, Malcolm Gladwell notes the research that supports the idea of giving kids a head start as it relates to later success in life.

Focuses on 16 of the most sought after leader qualities: If you analyze why leaders succeed and where they fail, you'll find that most can be summed up among core qualities we refer to as the "Sweet 16." These provide a strong foundation, by concentrating on the essentials. Half of these are character oriented and the other half skills.

Establishes a leader self-image: Because leadership is typically considered an adult activity in our culture, most kids do not see themselves as leaders. Trainers and parents attest to the observable change in disposition as they gain confidence and begin to think of themselves differently.

Get noticed by prime universities and employers: Competition for key college education and good paying jobs is increasing. More and more universities are looking beyond GPA/SAT/ACT scores, seeking more well-rounded candidates who exhibit leadership qualities.

Executive quality training at sports and arts lesson prices: *Lead*Now training is modeled after some of the finest (and most expensive) executive training programs in the country, but age and price sized so that most families can afford to provide top tier training.

Growing Great Parents of Leaders

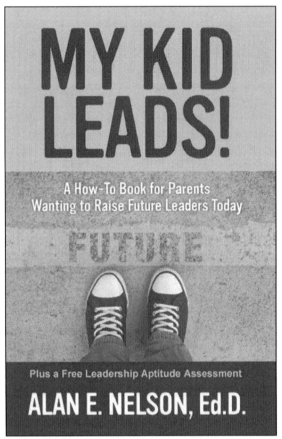

We highly encourage you to read the 199-page book, "My Kid Leads!" You can also purchase it at Amazon.com and it is available in the *Kindle* format. Email us at info@kidlead.com for bulk discounts.

This book is packed with important and practical information that will help you better understand the uniqueness of young leaders, along with ideas for developing skills around the home.

The book consists of 44-easy-to-read chapters that you can select in any order you like. Pick what interests you.

In addition to this book, we continue to provide articles and information on our website that will help you as a parent to improve your leader development skills.

Thanks for believing in young leader development. You're changing the future and thereby history, through your young leader.

www.kidlead.com

The Story Behind LeadYoung. *Training Systems*

The founder of KidLead Inc. and developer of **Lead**Young Training Systems, is Alan E. Nelson, EdD. While pastoring for 20 years and starting two churches, Alan focused on leadership development for adults. But he came to the realization that adult leaders don't change much. Since leaders shape society and make history, he started wondering what it would be like to adapt executive caliber training methods and content, for leaders while they are young and more pliable.

Along with a team of others, Dr. Nelson designed **Lead**Young Training Systems. They saw such great results that he decided to begin a non-profit organization in the US called KidLead Inc. His work is now used around the world and he's considered a global expert in young leader development and a pioneer in the field.

LeadYoung Training Systems involve a series of age and stage programs, based on developmental levels of young leaders. Each focuses on the same 16 enduring qualities of effective and ethical leading, but with different emphases.

KiddieLead Lead1st.   *Ages 2-9 (Conditioning & Character)*

LeadNow.   *Ages 10-13 (Character & Competency)*

LeadWell.   *Ages 14-18 (Competency & Confidence)*

LeadStrong.   *Ages 19-23 (Confidence & Connections)*

Thanks again for believing in the importance of young leader development. Operating as a non-profit, 501.c.3 organization in the United States, we welcome private donations, corporate sponsors, and opportunities to pursue grants, in order to fund further research, scholarships, and Trainer certification.

Our vision is to identify and develop hundreds of thousands of leaders globally, who'll learn to be effective and ethical, because we got to them while they're still moldable (not moldy). We partner with training and youth organizations to provide the finest organizational leadership resources for young leaders.

For more information on our work, please contact us at www.kidlead.com.

If you want to change the world, focus on leaders.

If you want to change leaders, focus on them when they're young.

-Alan E. Nelson

Made in United States
Troutdale, OR
04/06/2024

19000449R00029